The Adventures of Sammy the Shark

Liar, Liar, Fins on fire!

K. W. LUMLEY

DEDICATION

I dedicate these stories to my children; If not for them I wouldn't have the driving force behind me. Dad loves you very much!

CONTENTS

Acknowledgments

Liar, Liar, Fins on fire

ACKNOWLEDGMENTS

Shannon,
For Believing in me. And pushing me to peruse my
dream.

1 LIAR, LIAR, FINS ON FIRE

Hi, My name is Sammy.
And today was not a good day.

Why was today not a good day?
Well I'll tell ya!

Today I got in trouble for lying!

Do ya know what lying is?
Let me tell ya.
Lying is saying something that is not true.

Have ya ever lied?

Well, let me tell ya about how I got in trouble for
lying.

This morning I had my friend Tommy over to play,
And we were wrestling inside the house, laughing and
having fun.

Then I knocked over the table in the dining room, and
broke Miss Shelley's favorite Crystal Starfish.
One of the points broke off.

We cleaned up the mess as fast as we could.
But the statue was broken.

What should I do?

Well I took the point , and put it back on his crystal arm.
And it stayed in place.
We hurried up and went outside to play.
I hoped no one would notice.

Tommy had to go home for dinner, So I went inside to wash my fins for dinner.

And guess what?
No one had noticed the broken statue yet!

I was in my room getting ready for bed, When Miss Shelley swam into my room. She was holding the statue in both fins. Before she could say anything...

"Tommy, did it", I said before I could stop myself.

Why did I say Tommy broke it, when it was me that broke it?

Was I afraid?

Maybe I didn't want to get in trouble.
Maybe I didn't know what to do!

So what did I do?
I Lied!!

Miss Shelley said, "Okay" And called Mrs. Bluegills,
Tommy's mommy.

The next day at school I saw Tommy. His desk is right
next to mine in class.

"Good morning Tommy" I said to him.

"I'm not talking to you Sammy Shark." Tommy said,
"You lied and said I broke the Statue, and it was you
that broke it."

"I didn't tell anyone that.", I said, knowing that
wasn't true.

"Your mom called my mom yesterday and said that I
broke her statue and tried to make it look like it
wasn't broken.", Tommy said.

"And if you didn't tell her that. Who did?", Tommy

asked.

"It was Coral that told, I heard her telling Ms. Shelley right before she called your mom.", I told him.

(Oh no, Coral didn't tell on Tommy. I just lied again.)

Do you know why I said that?

I'm not sure why I lied again.

I thought about that some more, but just shrugged my fins. At least Tommy wasn't mad at me, I decided.

At recess Tommy, me and some other kids were playing in the sandbox, When Coral came out to play.

She looked all around until she saw us all playing in the sandbox, She smiled and swam over to where we were playing.
When she got to the sandbox she smile and waved and said "hello".

"Hi everyone can I play too?", Coral asked politely.

Tommy looked at her and gave her a very mean look.

"Come on guys let's go play over here, without Coral!", Tommy said, and started to swim away.

That made me feel very bad, because I could tell it hurt Corals feelings.

"Why can't I come play with you?", Coral asked.

Tommy said, "Because you might see one of us do something and tell on us and get us in trouble like you did to me!"

"No I won't!", Coral said," Why would I do something like that? I never told on you Tommy!"

"Liar, liar, fin's on fire tail's as long as a fisherman's wire!"

"Tommy, I never told on you I promise.", Coral cried.

"Liar, liar, fin's on fire tail's as long as a fisherman's wire!", Tommy sang·
And the other kids joined in with him!

This was too much for Coral, she burst into tears, and tried to swim away·
But they wouldn't let her, where ever she swam they followed her singing their hurtful song·

"Liar, liar, fin's on fire tail's as long as a fisherman's wire!"

"Liar, liar, fin's on fire tail's as long as a fisherman's wire!"

"Liar, liar, fin's on fire tail's as long as a fisherman's wire!"

The Recess shell whistled, and recess was over·

When the kids teasing Coral heard the shell whistle·
They stopped following Coral, and started to swim back to class· But still singing their song all the way back to the school·

"Liar, liar, fin's on fire tail's as long as a fisherman's

wire!"

"Liar, liar, fin's on fire tail's as long as a fisherman's wire!"

We all made it back to class, and back to our daily school lessons. But I couldn't pay attention. I couldn't stop thinking about what happened to Coral.

It was all my fault, all because I couldn't tell the truth about me breaking the statue.

I was in our kitchen eating some yummy sardines and drinking a glass of squid ink.
When I heard Coral get home from school.

"What's the matter, Coral?", I heard Ms. Shelley ask.

"Today at school Tommy.", she started to say.

I could tell she was very upset by the sound of her voice.

But I didn't stay to hear what she was saying.

Why didn't I stay to hear?

I already knew what she saying.
She was telling her about how Tommy had teased her.

So I went outside to play in my sandcastle clubhouse
my dad built for me. I tried to play, but I couldn't
have any fun.

Why couldn't I have fun?

I kept thinking about Coral, and what she told Ms.
Shelley.

Was I scared?

Yes, it made me a little bit scared.
What if they found out I broke the statue and lied
about it.
What if they found out the reason Tommy was mean
at school to Coral, was because I lied to Tommy.
I would be in very big trouble.

I was playing in the yard for a little while, When Ms.
Shelley came outside and said she wanted to talk to
me.

"I just got off the phone with Tommy's mom.", she

said to me.

"Do ya know what Tommy's mommy told me?", She asked.

"Nope." I said.

"Well, Come inside and we can talk about it.", she said.

Do you know what she wanted to talk to me about?

You are probably right, about Coral or lying.

I followed her into the living room. And I was very surprised by what I saw.

What do you think I saw in our living room.
You will never guess so I will tell you.

It was Coral and Ms. Shelley, and Tommy and His mommy, Mrs. Bluegills.
All of them where in my living room.
Ms. Shelley looked very upset.
All of them looked like they were mad at me.

"Hello.", I said.

"Is there anything you want to tell us Sammy, Anything about the statue?", Ms. Shelley asked.

I was very afraid, I didn't want to get into trouble.

"Tommy didn't break your statue." I said, "it was me."

I felt so bad about what I did. And started to cry. And I explained everything that happened.

"I see." Ms. Shelley said,"I'm very disappointed in you Sammy."

"I think you should go to your room.", She told me," And wait in there until I come in and talk to you."

So I swam off to my room, with my head hanging low, as I wiped the tears from my face with my fin.

Coral and Tommy why don't you kids go play in the yard while I talk to Mrs. Bluegills.

"okay.", They both said, And went outside.

I could Ms. Shelley and Mrs. Bluegills talking after the

others had gone outside.

I heard Ms. Shelley say" That I should have admitted to breaking the statue."

"Yes, he probably should have. But I think Sammy feels horrible about it, don't be too hard on him." Mrs. Bluegills said.

"Yes, I know he feels bad about it. He will have enough trouble making it all up to Tommy and Coral.", Said Ms. Shelley.

They both laughed a little.

I heard her saying that she was very sorry, and that I would be punished for lying.

Tommy stayed and played with Coral outside for quite some time.

While I waited in my room I watched them playing outside through my bedroom window. They were playing leap frog, that's one of my favorite games.

Was I nervous?
Yes, I knew I was in serious trouble.

Ms. Shelley came back into my room and sat on the edge of my bed.

"Sammy.", She said, "come sit beside me."

So I did.

"Sammy, do you know why lying was wrong?", she asked me," Do you understand everything that you did?"

I nodded and hid my face, she put her fin under my chin and lifted my face so I could look at her.

"Listen to me Sammy." She told me

Do you know what she told me?
Well I'll tell ya.

"Lying is wrong, and telling the truth is important." She said," How can we believe what you tell us if we find out you have been lying?"

"When we ask you anything, We have to know that the things you tell us are right and true.",she said.

"Lying got Tommy in trouble when he didn't do anything wrong.", she said.

"Lying to Tommy ,made him mad at Coral, he was very mean to her at school, do you know that he made her cry?" she asked.

I Nodded, and didn't say anything.

"And now they are both very mad at you." she said. "How does that make you feel Sammy?"

Do you know how that made me feel?
Want me to tell you?

I told Ms. Shelley, " It makes me feel very bad, I got my best friends into trouble by lying, I got my sister teased and made fun of because I lied."

"Now, everyone hate me, because I am a liar!", I said, and started to cry again.

"No one hates you Sammy.", She said softly, "We are disappointed in you, but we don't hate you, We love you."

Do know what she did next?
She Leaned over and kissed my forehead and whispered
something to me.

Do you know what she whispered to me?
I'll tell ya.

She said, "Sammy you are grounded for the next two
weeks."

Do you know what that means?

That means no sandbox, no swimming outside, no
playing with friends.

No fun at all!

So do you understand why lying is wrong?
Because lying makes your friends and family not believe
what you say , because they can't trust you.

Lying got my best friend in trouble, and made him not
like me.

Do you know how I should fix this?

Should I go tell Tommy and Coral I am sorry?

Should I tell the truth from now on?

You are right.

I will tell the truth from now on. I don't want my friends to not like me.
I don't want my parents to be disappointed in me.
I want to be trusted.
I don't want to get my friends into trouble for something I did.
And I never want to make my sister cry because my lying made the other kids tease her.

Whelp, I'm grounded and I gotta go,

Remember have fun, and try not to lie.

It will get you into trouble.

And see ya in two weeks!!

www.ingramcontent.com/pod-product-compliance
Lightning Source LLC
Chambersburg PA
CBHW030013040426
42337CB00012BA/768